Citified!

Paris

by Jessica Rudolph

Consultant: Karla Ruiz, MA
Teachers College, Columbia University
New York, New York

BEARPORT
PUBLISHING

New York, New York

Credits

Cover, © TTstudio/Shutterstock; TOC Top, © Nitr/Shutterstock; TOC Bottom, © Tupungato/Shutterstock; 4–5, © maziarz/Shutterstock; 7, © DOELAN Yann/Hemis/Alamy Stock Photo; 8, © Tom Roche/Shutterstock; 9, © ASIFE/iStock; 10, © pichetw/Shutterstock; 11T, Public Domain; 11B, © muratart/Shutterstock; 12L, © Guillermo Pis Gonzalez/Shutterstock; 12–13, © Dirk Wenzel/Dreamstime; 14, © kan_khampanya/Shutterstock; 15, © Eric Chan/CC BY 4.0; 16, © Tupungato/Shutterstock; 17T, © Nikonaft/Shutterstock; 17B, © AA World Travel Library/Alamy Stock Photo; 18–19, © Brian Kinney/Shutterstock; 19B, © Jose Ignacio Soto/Shutterstock; 20T, © Jordan Lye/Shutterstock; 20BL, © sam74100/iStock; 20BR, © Visionsi/Shutterstock; 21T, © Paola Crash/Shutterstock; 21B, © Carlo Bollo/Alamy Stock Photo; 22 (Clockwise from Top Right), © PHOTOCREO Michal Bednarek/Shutterstock, © pichetw/Shutterstock, © Anna Kucherova/Shutterstock, © Vit Kovalcik/Shutterstock, and © WDG Photo/Shutterstock; 23 (T to B), © Viacheslav Lopatin/Shutterstock, © meunierd/Shutterstock, © Jose Ignacio Soto/Shutterstock, © Alexey Seleznev/Shutterstock, © Stas Guk/Shutterstock, and © goodluz/Shutterstock; 24, © ESB Professional/Shutterstock.

Publisher: Kenn Goin
Editor: J. Clark
Creative Director: Spencer Brinker
Photo Researcher: Thomas Persano

Library of Congress Cataloging-in-Publication Data

Names: Rudolph, Jessica, author.
Title: Paris / by Jessica Rudolph.
Description: New York, New York : Bearport Publishing, 2018. | Series: Citified! | Audience: Ages 5 to 8. | Includes bibliographical references and index.
Identifiers: LCCN 2017005120 (print) | LCCN 2017010869 (ebook) | ISBN 9781684022335 (library bound) | ISBN 9781684022878 (ebook)
Subjects: LCSH: Paris (France)—Juvenile literature.
Classification: LCC DC707 .R84 2018 (print) | LCC DC707 (ebook) | DDC 944/.361—dc23
LC record available at https://lccn.loc.gov/2017005120

For more information, write to Bearport Publishing Company, Inc., 45 West 21st Street, Suite 3B, New York, New York 10010. Printed in the United States of America.

10 9 8 7 6 5 4 3 2 1

Contents

Welcome to
PARIS
The City of Lights!

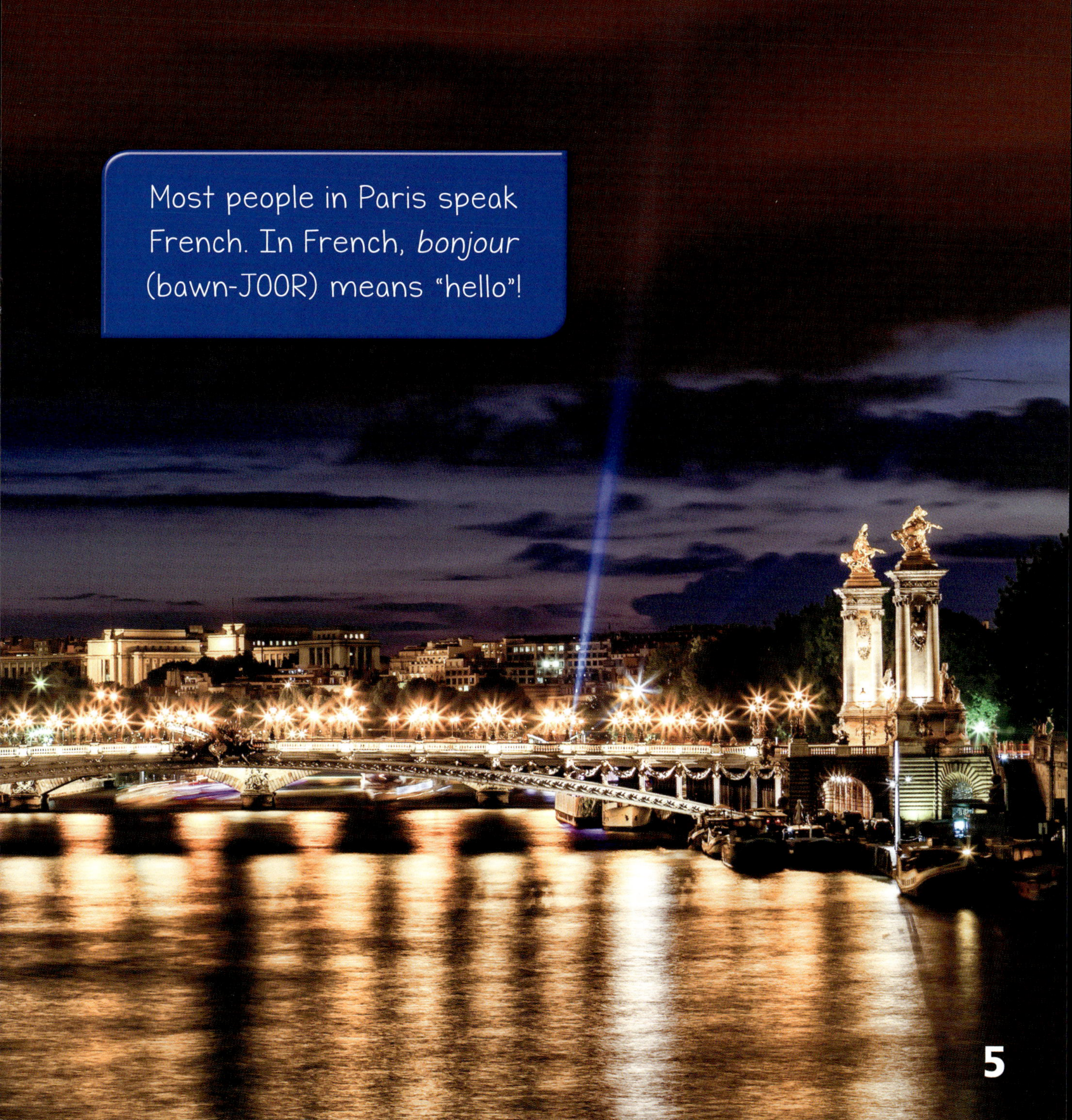

Most people in Paris speak French. In French, *bonjour* (bawn-JOOR) means "hello"!

Paris is the largest city in France.

More than two million people live there!

Paris is also the **capital** of France.

The Eiffel Tower is the tallest structure in the city.

It rises 984 feet (300 m)!

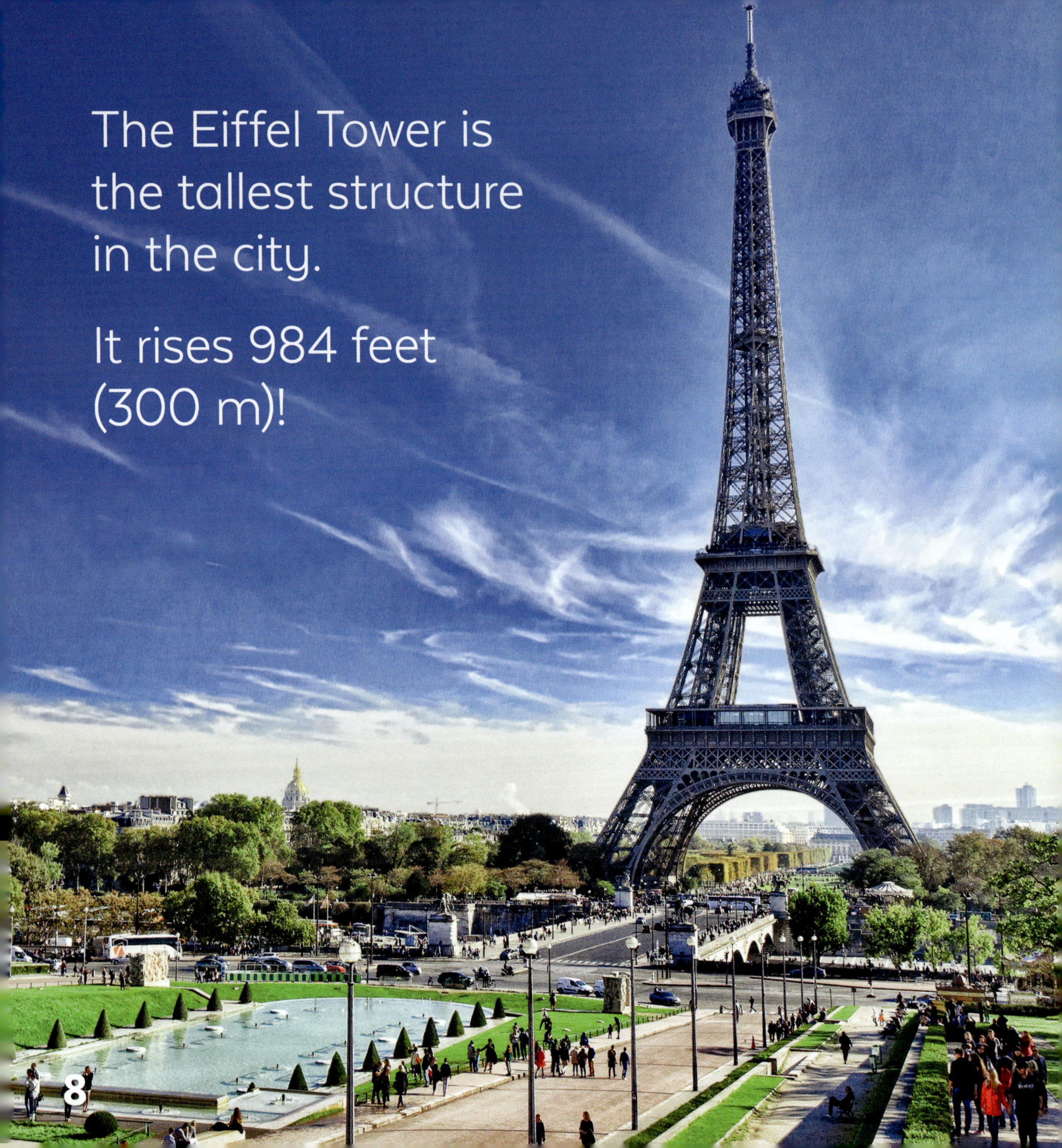

Tourists take elevators up to the top of the tower. There, they can look out over the city.

Paris has lots of art museums.

The Louvre (LOOV) shows 35,000 works of art.

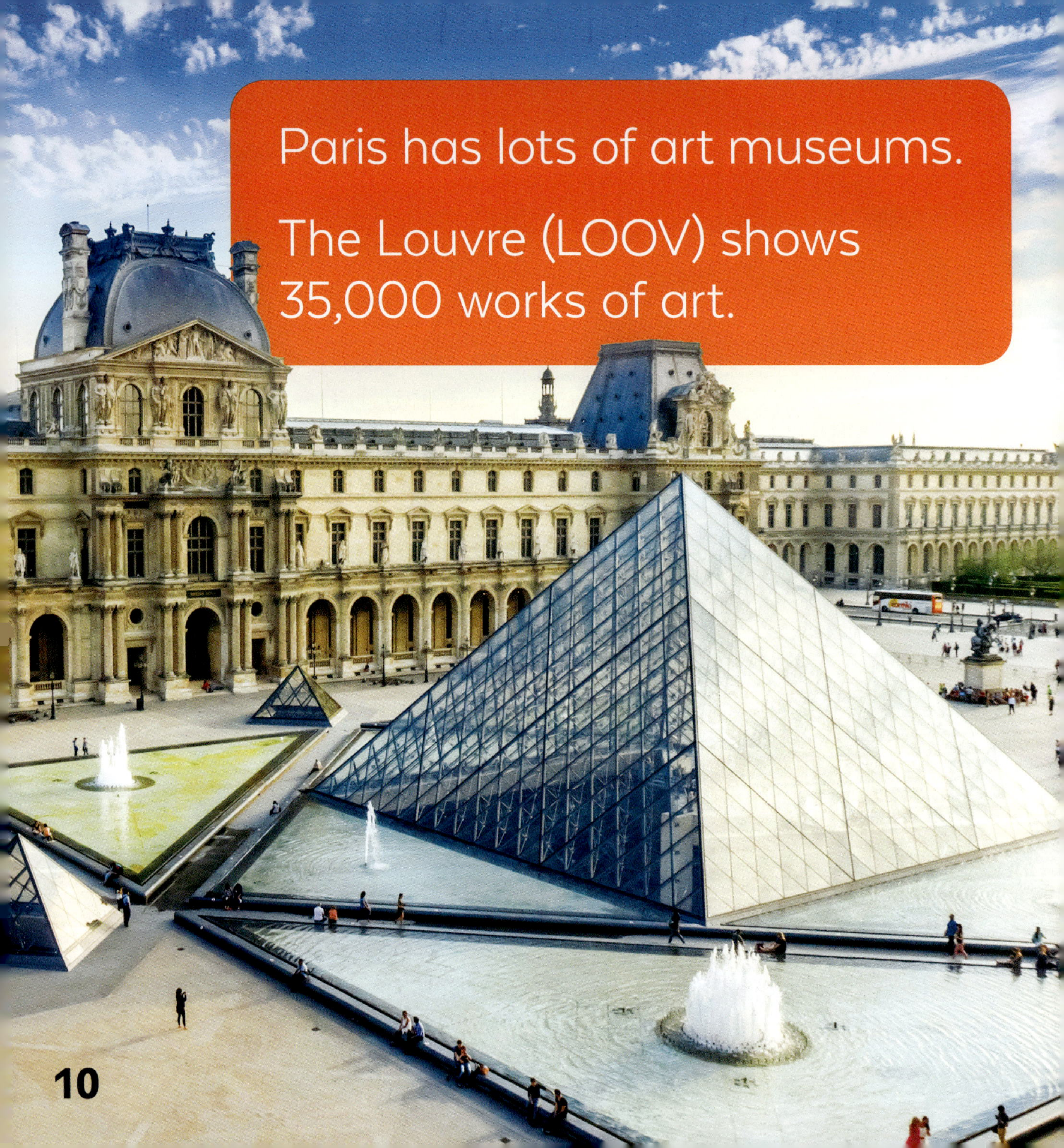

The museum's most popular painting is the *Mona Lisa*.

People crowd around her!

An Italian artist named Leonardo da Vinci painted the *Mona Lisa* in 1503.

If you have the nerve, visit the Catacombs.

This burial place was built in the 1700s.

Underground tunnels are lined with human bones and skulls!

The Catacombs hold the **remains** of more than six million people!

The Arc de Triomphe is a famous **monument**.

It was built in the early 1800s to honor the French army.

People can climb 284 steps to get to the top of the monument.

The Jardin du Luxembourg is a special place for children.

It's a huge garden where kids can play with toy sailboats!

Children can also watch puppet shows and ride a merry-go-round at the garden.

Notre Dame is a
huge church in Paris.

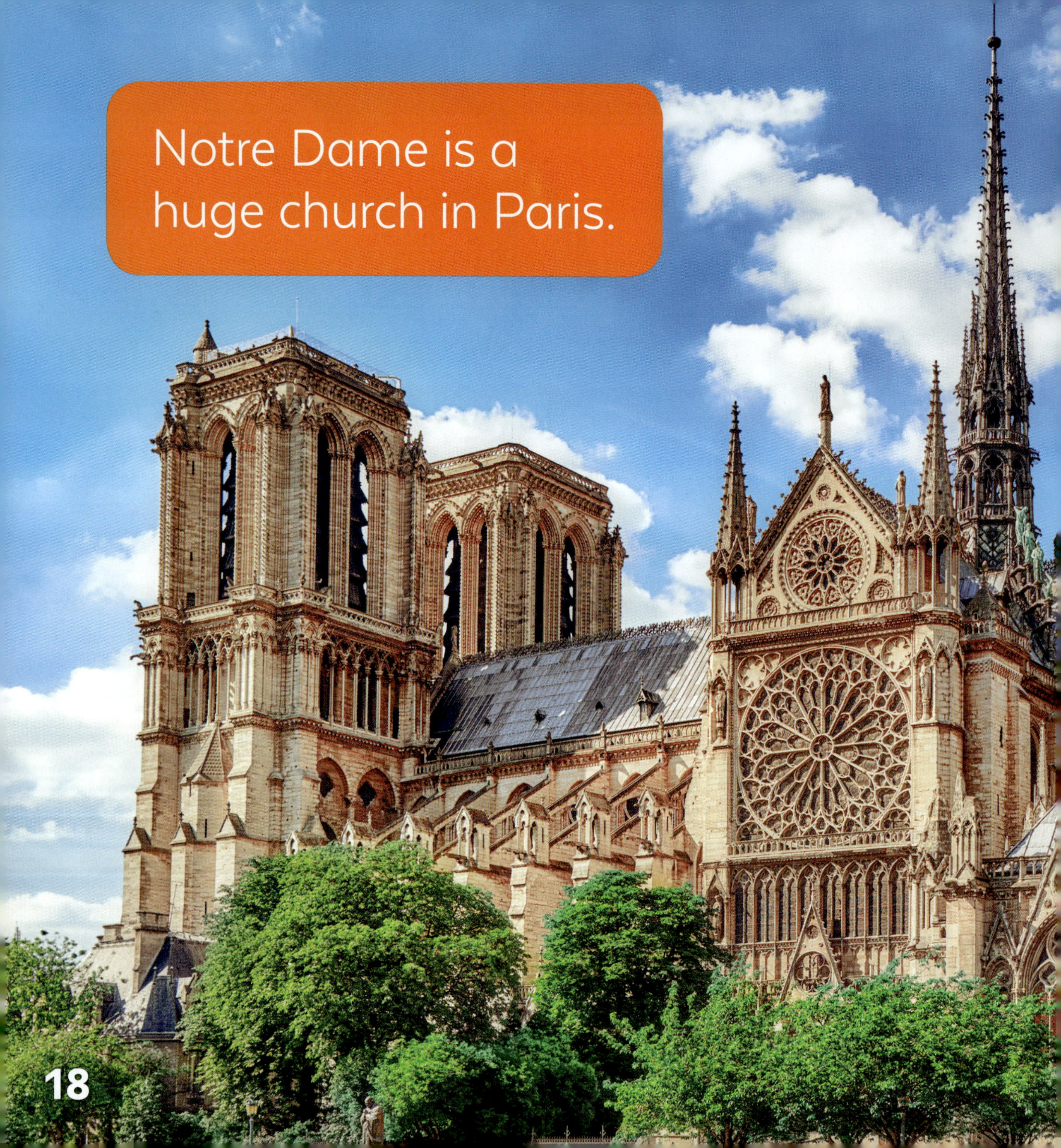

It's located on a tiny island along the Seine River.

People admire the church's beautiful **architecture**.

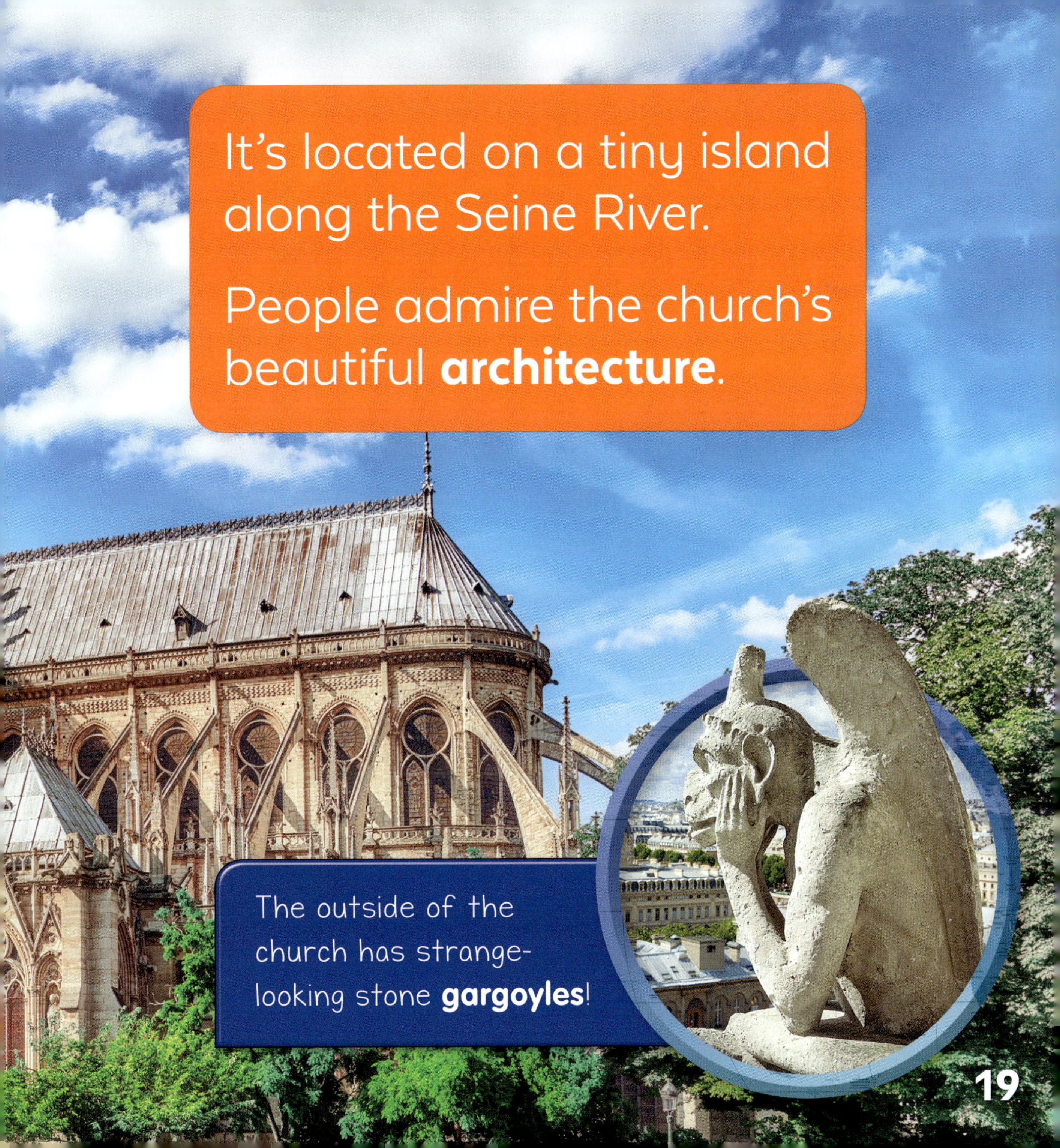

The outside of the church has strange-looking stone **gargoyles**!

For a treat, head into a chocolate shop.

In Paris, desserts can be works of art!

Try chocolate cake, a chocolate bar, or an éclair.

Yum!

A person who makes or sells chocolate is called a *chocolatier*.

MAP IT!

Paris

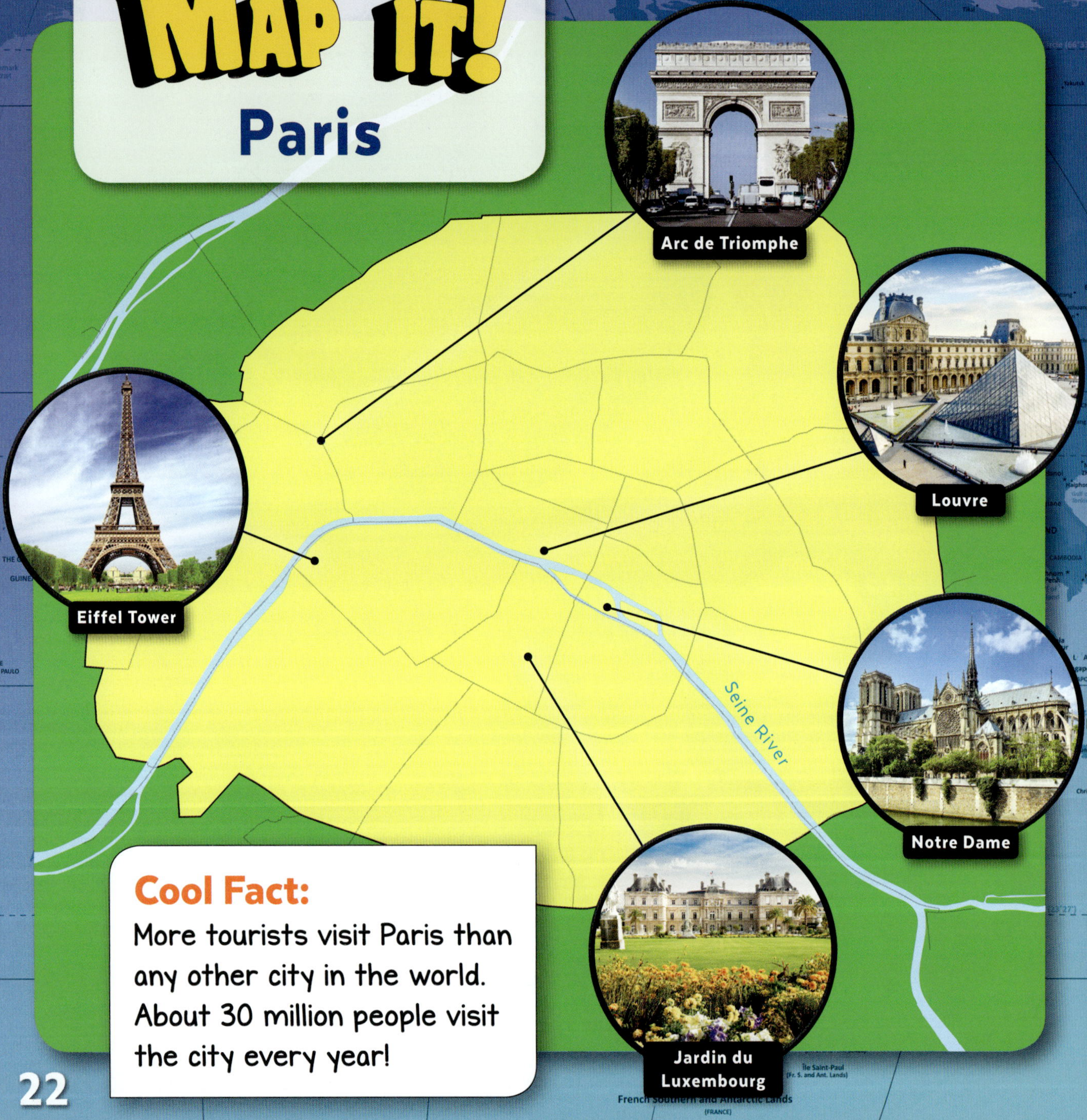

Cool Fact:

More tourists visit Paris than any other city in the world. About 30 million people visit the city every year!

Glossary

architecture (AR-kuh-tek-chur) a style or method of designing buildings

capital (KAP-uh-tuhl) a city where a country's government is based

gargoyles (GAR-goylz) waterspouts in the form of frightening humans or animal figures sticking out of rooftops

monument (MAHN-yoo-muhnt) a structure built to honor a person or an event

remains (rih-MAYNZ) what is left of a body after death

tourists (TOOR-ists) people who travel to and visit places for pleasure

Index

Read More

Rubbino, Salvatore. *A Walk in Paris.* Somerville, MA: Candlewick Press (2014).

Sasek, Miroslav. *This Is Paris.* New York: Universe Publishing (2004).

Learn More Online

To learn more about Paris, visit
www.bearportpublishing.com/Citified

About the Author

Jessica Rudolph has written many books about history, science, and nature for children. Her favorite part of visiting Paris was touring the creepy Catacombs.